TREASURE HUNT

Sean Callery

Published 2011 by
A&C Black Publishers Ltd.
36 Soho Square, London, W1D 3QY

www.acblack.com

ISBN   HB 978-1-4081-3355-2
       PB 978-1-4081-3358-3

Text copyright © 2010 Sean Callery

This book is produced using paper that is made from wood grown in managed, sustainable forests. It is natural, renewable and recyclable. The logging and manufacturing processes conform to the environmental regulations of the country of origin.

Produced for A&C Black by Calcium. www.calciumcreative.co.uk

Printed and bound in China by C&C Offset Printing Co.

All the internet addresses given in this book were correct at the time of going to press. The author and publishers regret any inconvenience caused if addresses have changed or sites have ceased to exist, but can accept no responsibility for any such changes.

Acknowledgements

The publishers would like to thank the following for their kind permission to reproduce their photographs:

Cover: Shutterstock
Pages: Dreamstime: Erik Gauger 10, Witold Krasowski 18, Mitja Mladkovic 1, 5t; Shutterstock: Alfredolon 21, Galina Barskaya 4, Bobby Deal/RealDealPhoto 13, Eric Gevaert 19, Fer Gregory 12, Anna Jurkovska 16, Eduard Kyslynskyy 11, Myotis 15, Lobke Peers 8, Sakala 6, Jozef Sedmak 9, Dani Simmonds 14, Zoran Vukmanov Simokov 7, Sandra van der Steen 17, Tatjana Strelkova 3, 20, SueC 5b.

Contents

Hop On Board

I am **Captain** Black. This is the story of one of my greatest treasure hunts ever.

Look at that ship!
One day at sea, I spotted a huge ship. "Raise the Jolly Roger!" I shouted.

I told my **crew** to attack.

4

We'll fight you

The Jolly Roger was a pirate **flag**. It told people that the **pirates** would fight.

Attack!

There was no treasure on the big ship. But we did find a **treasure map** – hurrah!

Take it all

We didn't just take the map. We stole the ship too!

Give me your ship

We pirates were great fighters.

Treasure hunters

Pirates hunted for treasure such as jewels, gold, and silver.

Treasure

Treasure!

The treasure map showed an island. It was marked with an X – for treasure.

Let's go

"There's **loot** there!" I told my crew. We **voted** to sail for the island straight away.

Treasure maps were drawn by hand.

8

Hands up

Pirates voted by raising their hands if they agreed.

X marks the spot

Danger Island

Then we sailed to the island. As we waded to the shore, a crocodile bit me on the leg.

Cook and doctor

Our cook patched up my leg. Pirate cooks didn't just cook – they were the ships' doctors too.

Look out for crocs

Don't go in the water

Pirates had to watch out for lots of dangerous sea creatures.

A perfect treasure island.

Dig, Me Hearties!

Next we reached the spot marked X on the map. "Dig!" I shouted to my pirate crew.

Found it!

As we dug, our spades hit something hard. Then we saw a wooden chest. I knew the treasure must be inside.

Pirates hid their treasure in chests.

We're all rich

Pirates always shared treasure. But the captain got the most!

Treasure chest

What is inside?

Lovely Loot

Bang! Joe fired his **pistol** at the lock and it snapped open. The chest was full of coins.

Money, money, money

Inside the chest we saw lots of gold coins. They were called **doubloons**.

Treasure

Doubloon

Cut up coins

Silver coins that could be cut up to share were called 'pieces of eight'.

Never come between a pirate and his treasure!

Over Here!

Then Ben lit a bonfire so our **shipmates** left on the ship could see where we were.

No mobile phones...
We pirates didn't have phones or radios. We used flags, fires, or even trumpets to send messages.

Bonfire

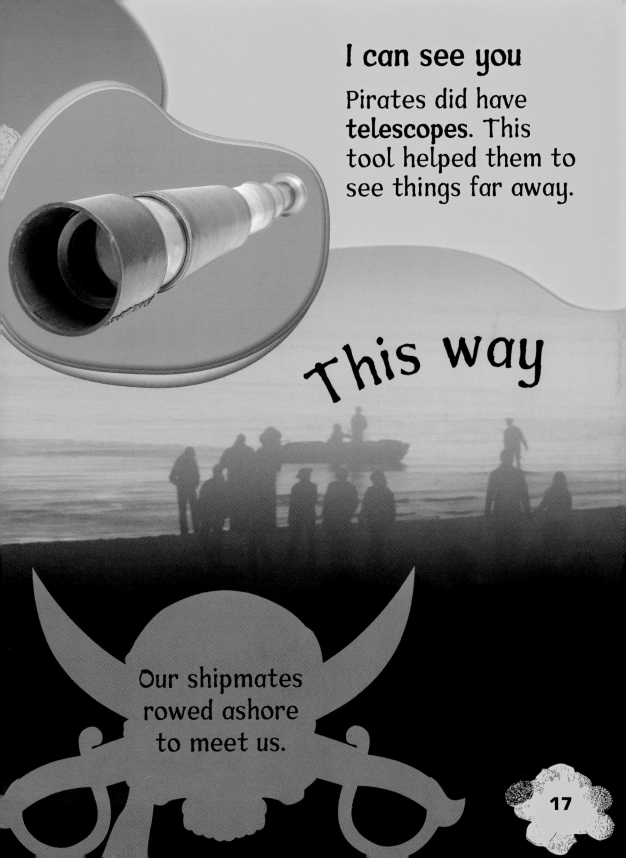

I can see you

Pirates did have **telescopes**. This tool helped them to see things far away.

This way

Our shipmates rowed ashore to meet us.

Load Up

We filled the boat with treasure.
Ben said he would row it to the ship.
He promised to come back for us.

A pirate's life

We all needed that treasure.
Once you are a pirate, you
can't get a normal job!

Ben took the
treasure back
to our ship.

Pirate pets

Although pirates were tough, they still kept pets such as monkeys.

See you!

19

The End?

Can you believe it? Ben sailed away without us. Arghhhh!

Island life

We were left alone on the island, with no ship and no treasure. Ben had taken the lot.

Pirates fought to the death for treasure.

We'll get him

If we ever catch Ben, we'll dump him on an island. Hang on, that's what he has done to us!

Just you wait, Ben

Glossary

captain person who is in charge of a ship and its crew

crew pirates and sailors who work on a ship

doubloons Spanish gold coins

flag piece of material with a pattern or picture

loot money, jewels, or other things that pirates stole from ships

pirates robbers who stole from ships

pistol small gun

shipmates sailors or pirates who belonged to the same crew

telescopes tools that help people to see things far away

treasure map drawing that showed pirates where to go

voted chose

Further Reading

Websites

Read all about pirates and try out some fun games at:
http://nationalgeographic.com/pirates

There is lots of information about pirates at:
www.thekidswindow.co.uk/News/Pirates.htm

Books

Pirate by Deborah Lock, Dorling Kindersley (2005).

Pirates: Rogues' Gallery by John Matthews, Carlton Books (2007).

Why Did Pirates Bury Treasure? by Catherine Chambers, Miles Kelly (2005).

Index